The Little Ang

Who's Afraid of the Dark?

Written & Illustrated
by Leia A. Stinnett

Cover art by Leia Stinnett

ISBN 0-929385-89-6

Published by
StarChild Press
a division of

Light Technology
Publishing
P.O. Box 1526
Sedona, Arizona 86339
(520) 282-6523

Printed by
**MISSION
POSSIBLE**
Commercial
Printing

P.O. Box 1495
Sedona, AZ 86339

A NOTE TO PARENTS

This is a book about fear. Fear is something most every person on Earth has faced or is presently facing in their life. We are afraid of illness, of death, of losing our jobs, of not being successful, of not being good enough, of not finding happiness.

We are afraid of so many things that we create a lot of darkness in our lives, along with unhappiness and other negative thoughts, feelings and beliefs.

Fear is an absence of light. When you are afraid, it is important to remember that within each of us is the light of God. We are each a part of a greater whole, the source of All That Is. We can use this light as protection. We can use this light to change our lives.

We create our own fears and we can create our own light – from that light within. Remember, where there is light there is no darkness; where there is no darkness there can be no fear.

This is a story about healing fear. Each of us must face our own monsters and dissolve them in light.

Peter was afraid of the dark. In his imagination, he created ugly monsters lurking in the shadows of his room, waiting to pounce on him the moment he closed his eyes and went to sleep.

To Peter, every shadow was something to fear. He wasn't always sure about what was hiding in those shadows, but he knew — he just knew — it meant trouble for him the moment he let his guard down.

When Peter was told to go to bed, he would run into the

1

bathroom and hide out, or attempt to hide out by taking an extra long bath, brushing his teeth six times or more and washing his face until it was bright pink and tender to the touch.

After a period of time Peter's mother would open the door and order him off to bed, much to his disappointment.

Peter tried to coax his mother to leave the light on in his room each night. He would promise her that he would turn it off in a short time, that he had to finish some homework or read a chapter of his favorite story.

But she would insist on turning out the light, after assuring him and reassuring him that there was nothing to be afraid of, that the angels would protect him.

Then, she would add, "Peter, the sooner you go to sleep, the sooner the Sun can come out and it won't be nighttime any longer!"

Yes, Peter knew that night passes quickly once you go to sleep, but it's that part about going to sleep that bothered him.

Peter waited until he heard his mom reach the bottom of the stairs. Quietly he would turn the light back on and snuggle back down under his warm comforter. It seemed that Peter's mom could see with x-ray vision right into Peter's room.

Just like magic, Mom always seemed to know when Peter had turned the light back on. She would either march right back up the stairs and angrily turn off the light, or Peter would hear her shout at him from the base of the stairs, "Peter, turn out that light . . . right *now!*"

So out went the light . . . very reluctantly. Peter's imagination began to run wild the moment the lights went out. He pulled the blankets up under his nose allowing only his eyes and the top of his head to be exposed to whatever was lurking in his room.

Whenever he heard a sound or saw a shadow on the wall, he quickly yanked the bedcovers up over the top of his head.

But curiosity usually got the best of Peter. He very cautiously drew the covers back down under his nose, his eyes carefully scanning his room. What was in the room tonight? What kinds of things were waiting for him to drift off into sleep and then pounce on him . . . and . . .

Oh, no! It was all so horrible! Peter never could figure out completely what the "things" in the night would do to him. He really didn't want to ever find out!

Peter liked to watch television after school when his parents were at work. He seemed to be drawn to watch science fiction movies, horror movies, movies where people were attacked by lions and tigers and such. Most of the pictures he watched showed monsters and other such creatures lurking around at night . . . in the dark.

Peter would imagine that there were monsters and ugly creatures under his bed. He was afraid to get out of bed to go to the bathroom. He was always

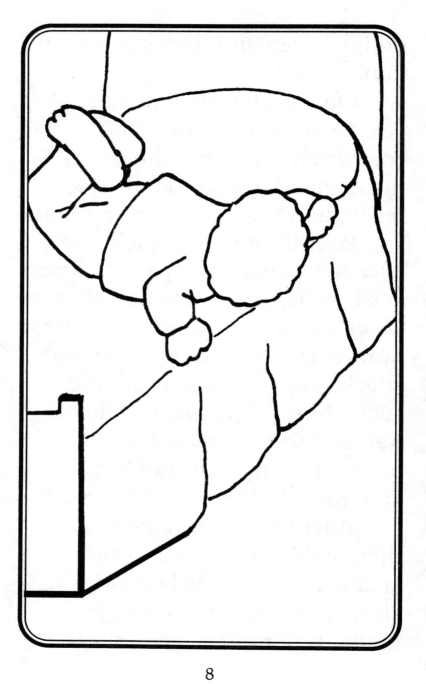

afraid that something ugly was going to grab his leg if he got out of bed in the dark.

He remembered that when he was very, very small he would get up out of bed very often during the night. In order to get some sleep, his mother had told the small child that if he got up in the night the bad monster under his bed would get him.

From that time on that particular fear had been very real to Peter. Yes, he remembered that one and he did not want to find out if it was true or not.

Sometimes he would feel like peeking under the covers to see if there really was something under his bed. But the fear became too great. Peter decided it was not important to check out his

mother's story.

Peter was afraid of a lot of things. He had been told at school not to talk to strangers. His imagination often focused on the subject of "strangers" at night . . . in the dark.

"What if there is a stranger in my house . . . or in my room? What if he kidnaps me? What if he takes me far away and I never get to see my family ever again?

Peter's imagination took him one step further. "What if the stranger climbs the tree in front of my window and hides in my room until Mom makes me go to bed? What if he waits until the light goes out and then . . . ?"

Peter pulled the covers over his head at this point in his thoughts. He really didn't want to

know the rest of the story.

Peter's sleep time was filled with nightmares — dreams of people chasing him with knives and guns. He would see himself walking through the woods in his dream and a huge bear would pop out from behind a tree and run after him.

Peter would see himself swimming in the lake. Suddenly a huge shark would zoom to the surface in an effort to grab Peter's leg and drag him to the bottom of the murky lake.

Peter's nightmares were very real; they made him feel as though he were there, right in the middle of all the action — just like an actor in a television movie.

There were times when Peter saw himself in a horrible war,

bombs exploding all around him and then . . . *poof* . . . no more world, no more people.

Peter dreamed about fires, floods and earthquakes destroying his whole town. He often wondered what it would be like to live right in the middle of such an event.

In one dream Peter saw himself in his backyard, looking down a deep, dark hole. Suddenly he found himself falling, and he felt as though he were really falling into a bottomless pit.

Peter remembered waking up screaming for help.

Peter's dreams took him to faraway lands where he would encounter pirates with huge swords, Indians chasing after him with bows and arrows, gigantic space monsters pursuing him with laser weapons and ferocious lions and bears attempting to have him for dinner.

Peter was afraid of these dreams. He did not like seeing all these ugly things, all the monsters and horrible people trying to catch him.

Peter had one dream that really bothered him. He often wondered if it had anything to do with the camping trip he had gone on with his father and Uncle Foster.

Uncle Foster was a practical joker. He enjoyed scaring people and playing jokes on them.

Uncle Foster had special cans. When you took off the lid, a rubber snake would jump out — right in your face.

He also had a special black

box that made a sound like a moaning or whining noise. He really enjoyed playing this joke on the Halloween trick-or-treaters who came to his house each year. Usually they all ran away, forgetting all about their treats.

Peter and his father went camping in the woods, knowing only too well that Uncle Foster would try to scare them. Peter thought he was ready for anything Uncle Foster could dish out, but he was wrong.

The campers pitched their tent in a clearing in the woods, prepared a hearty meal over the blazing campfire, and then each took a comfortable seat on a log around the fire. Uncle Foster prepared to tell his famous ghost stories.

Storytime was Uncle Foster's

forte. He was well known all over town for his tall tales. He could keep a straight face no matter how funny the joke was that he was telling.

As the little group formed around the campfire, Uncle Foster began his tale about the huge creature who lived in the very spot where they had set up camp for the weekend. Peter began to shake and shudder as Uncle Foster began weaving his tale of horror.

Peter's eyes grew larger and larger. His face turned pale white. He began hearing noises, rustling noises in the bushes. Someone or something was coming closer into their camp!

Peter let out a loud scream, sending Uncle Foster into a round of uncontrolled laughter.

Peter didn't think it was funny at all. Peter was really upset with Uncle Foster, and even more upset with his dad, who proceeded to tell Uncle Foster all about Peter's fears.

Uncle Foster managed three more bedtime horror stories, and then acknowledged it was time to retire: "Let's all hit the hay, fellas!"

Each of the three took one corner of the tent, claiming their space with sleeping bags and toilet items. They changed into their nightwear and climbed into the sleeping bags. Peter zipped up his bag all the way to his neck.

"Please don't turn out the lantern, Dad," Peter begged. "Please leave it on in case I have to go to the bathroom!"

"Peter, if you need to go to

the bathroom, just turn on your flashlight and go on outside, over there behind the big log. There is nothing out there to be afraid of. It was only a story. Uncle Foster and I are right here! Go to sleep!" Peter's dad was firm.

Peter's father had grown up with very strict parents. His father, in particular, did not like anyone in his family to show any fear at all. Grandpa felt it was a sign of cowardice. Peter and his grandfather did not get along.

Uncle Foster continued laughing, poking fun at Peter, calling him a "sissy" in a teasing manner. Peter was very hurt by all of the heckling, but he refused to cry. He held back his emotions as best he could; but no matter what anyone tried to do or say, Peter had

to admit he was afraid of the dark.

So out went the light. Peter could see shadows dancing on the canvas from the flickering campfire outside. "Wild animals don't like fire," Peter assured himself. He remembered his father telling him that the first time they went camping together.

"The animals won't come into our camp as long as the fire . . . but what if the fire goes out while we sleep? Then what?"

Peter's fears were growing.

Before Peter could finish his thoughts, a creaking sound caught his attention. His body became rigid. What was that? he wondered, his eyes opening wide, his body shaking. There it is again! It sounded like footsteps. Was it the creature Uncle Foster talked about in his story? Was the story true?

"Dad, Dad, wake up! There's something outside. I hear something outside. Wake up! Quick, turn on the light!" Peter was pulling unmercifully at his father's sleeping bag.

His father opened his eyes, and although Peter could not see his father's face clearly, he just knew his father was angry for being awakened by what he defined as "Peter's senseless fears."

"Go . . . to . . . sleep. Go to sleep now!" demanded Peter's father.

"But Dad . . . ," Peter began.

"No, Peter, no light. Go to sleep. There is nothing out there. It is only the fire making a crackling noise. Go to sleep."

So Peter lay back down and pulled the sleeping bag up over his head. He looked like a mummy by the time he got done rearranging himself so no part of his body was showing to the outside world. After a while, he pushed the top part of the sleeping bag down under his chin.

Peter tried to close his eyes. But just as he started to close them, he would hear a sound or see a shadow dancing on the side of the tent. He knew something was out there waiting for him to fall asleep — probably that creature Uncle Foster was talking about in his story. Yep, it must be that creature.

Peter finally dropped off to sleep, too exhausted from his day's adventure to keep his eyes open

28

any longer. Peter awakened his
father and Uncle Foster four times
during the night. He had a
nightmare about the creature
Uncle Foster had mentioned in
his story. He heard noises. He
saw shadows. He felt things touch
his face.

Peter's imagination was
beginning to get out of hand.
Finally, morning arrived. Peter was
overjoyed at his first glimpse of the
Sun peeking over the top of the
tree above the tent. Peter was glad
they were only staying one night.
He had made up his mind he
would never come here again. No,
not him . . . ever!

Peter's father looked exhausted.
His face was very drawn. He was
very quiet, as though he had a lot
on his mind.

Peter had tossed and turned all night, letting out little moans and groans just about the time his father had drifted off to sleep. Peter's father had made up his mind never to bring Peter along on any more camping trips.

Peter felt bad about disturbing his father's sleep. But he couldn't help it. It wasn't his fault that Uncle Foster decided to tell ghost stories, especially the one about the creature in the woods. No, it wasn't Peter's fault.

Peter felt embarrassed, but he rationalized that his fears were real and was disappointed in his mother and father, and in Uncle Foster, for not believing his stories. He was afraid that one night one of those monsters would take him away, and then his parents would feel bad about not believing him in the first place.

Yes, it would be quite some time, thought Peter, before he would ever forget the camping trip in the old woods and that creature . . . out there somewhere. The creature appeared in many of Peter's nightmares. Peter did not know how to make it go away.

The following day Peter was very quiet. He tried to stay off by himself so he would not make his father any more angry than he already was.

The evening came much more quickly than Peter had wished for. "Oh no, another night. I haven't gotten over the past one yet. Now I gotta do it again!" Peter sounded disappointed.

Peter's mother followed her

usual routine. "It's time for bed, Peter, now!"

Tonight she added a few more words: "And be quick about it, Peter — no delays!" She sounded angry, too.

"What's wrong with Mom and Dad? Don't they understand what it feels like to be afraid? Haven't they ever been afraid of anything? I'm sure I am not the only person who's ever been afraid," Peter began sobbing quietly. He felt very, very alone.

Peter went through the process of taking a shower, brushing his teeth and hair and washing his face. He did not try to delay the inevitable. He dressed in his pajamas while thinking about all the shadows that would soon visit his room.

Peter climbed into bed. His

mother soon arrived to turn out his light and give him a good-night kiss. "Good night, Peter. Sleep well."

Who was she kidding? thought Peter. Sleep well? Who could sleep well when you had to be on your guard all night long against the shadows?

Peter pulled the covers over his head for a moment. Tonight seemed different. Peter wasn't sure for a moment what that meant.

As he drew the covers down from his eyes, he noticed a full Moon shining brightly through his open window. The gentle breeze was blowing the tree branches back and forth, with some rubbing against the side of the house. Peter imagined the shadows from the branches as arms reaching out to grab him.

No, I won't be afraid, Peter

assured himself.

But his consoling thoughts soon melted into the old pattern of fear as noises abounded within his room and outside his window. The shadows were back!

Peter watched helplessly as a small ball of white light suddenly streaked into his room. The light moved into the center of the bedroom and appeared to grow larger and larger . . . brighter and brighter.

Peter started to panic, What if Mom thinks I turned on the light again? Boy, will she be mad at me!

Peter tried not to think about the punishment that would come his way if Mom found out about this light.

Peter became more and more concerned about the light as it became more and more bright,

more intense. Soon the brilliant white light filled Peter's entire room.

Peter sat straight up in bed. Rubbing his eyes to see if he were dreaming, he acknowledged to himself that this was an incredible dream. If, in fact, it was a dream. What was going on here?

Peter thought for a moment. He wasn't afraid! He didn't exactly know why . . . but this time, he was not afraid.

There was something or someone in his room, but he was not afraid. He only felt a sensation of being safe, protected, a feeling as though someone was holding him in his/her arms and loving him, gently, tenderly.

Peter rubbed his eyes again. Still the light filled the space. "No, this isn't a dream. But it could just

be my imagination . . ."

Before Peter could finish his sentence a beautiful angel appeared, growing right out of the center of the ball of light.

The angel was very tall, with short brown hair and intense but loving eyes. There was a golden light radiating all around the body of this angel and it had golden wings.

Peter was determined to find out if the angel was a boy or a girl. He had been under the impression that all angels were girls. But this angel looked different. This angel looked like a boy angel. Should he dare ask?

Before Peter could speak, the angel said to Peter:

"Peter, I am Paul, your guardian angel. I am here to help

you. I am here to teach you about fear — what it is and how to change fear into love. It really is very simple. I will help you."

Peter's mouth dropped open in such a way one might think he was swallowing a whale! His eyes were fixed wide open in total surprise.

He couldn't speak, he couldn't move one muscle of his body. He was frozen, yet he was not afraid.

The angel continued:

"Peter, where I come from there is no darkness . . . only light, pure loving light from the source of All That Is.

"Here on Earth, you have light in which to do your work and darkness, or night in which to rest your body. But people of Earth have created a different kind of darkness — the darkness known

as fear.

"Imagine now, Peter, that you are in your room and it is completely dark. How do you feel? Here, let me show you how it feels."

The angel made the room totally dark. Soon, Peter's fears returned.

"Oh . . . well . . ." It took Peter a moment to regain his ability to speak, to move his body.

"It scares me. I don't know what is in my room because I can't see," Peter responded to Paul's question.

"Now," Paul continued, "suppose you turn on your light. Here, I'll show you."

Paul turned his glowing light back on, filling Peter's entire room once again with the glorious light.

LONELINESS
FAILURE
PAIN
ILLNESS
FEARS
DEATH
LOSS
NO ONE LOVES ME!

"All right, Peter, how do you feel now?" Paul was looking lovingly at Peter.

"Well, I feel much better, 'cause now I can see my whole room. When the light goes on, all the shadows, all the monsters go away. They don't like the light," Peter stated proudly.

"Peter, the only monsters that exist are the monsters you make up in your imagination, the things you create from fear.

"People are afraid of lots of things: they fear getting sick, many people are afraid of dying, some people are afraid of losing their jobs, their homes, all their nice things.

"There are some people who are afraid they will not succeed in their chosen careers, that they will

not be able to please their parents. Some people are afraid of God, afraid He/She will punish them if they do not follow His/Her laws.

"People are afraid of things they can't see — their future, for instance. Just like you, there a lot of people who are afraid of the dark.

"Remember when it was dark in your room, I turned on the light? Remember how you felt when the light went on?" asked Paul.

"Yes," responded Peter.

"Well, what I am going to teach you is how to turn on a very special light inside of you — God's light — a light that is always there, a light that makes you feel strong and protected no matter where you are, or how afraid you might feel.

"Imagine a beam of white light coming down from the source,

down through the top of your head and out the center of your chest. This is God's light. God's light can help you feel safe and protected all day and all night.

"Imagine the white light coming out of your heart center and wrapping all around you until you can imagine yourself safe inside a beautiful white bubble of light. This bubble is very strong. Nothing can come into this bubble unless you want it to.

"Then it is important to face your fears. But before you can face your fears, you must know what it is you are afraid of. When you know what it is you are afraid of you can look at your fear face to face, shine your light on the fear, send it love and it will go away."

Peter began listing all the

things he was afraid of from the shadows in his room to destruction of the Earth in a nuclear war.

"Peter, whatever you think in your mind," Paul continued, "you can make happen in your life. When you fear something, that fear grows stronger and stronger. The fear takes control of your whole life. You let your fears be in charge of you!"

Peter was absorbing every word Paul was sharing with him in that moment.

"When you think of God's love and light as your protection, when you use this love and light to shine right at you fear, your fear cannot exist. Imagine yourself wearing a suit of armor, carrying a very bright light. Imagine yourself very strong and tall, shining your light on all your fears, one at a time. What happens to your fears?"

Peter felt that the fears went away. But what about the creatures? he thought.

"The creatures are part of your imagination. When you can't see what is there, you let your imagination create things." Paul seemed to read the thoughts in Peter's mind as he spoke.

"Do not let your thoughts wander to what *might be* or what *could* happen. It is important for you to think about how special you are, what a beautiful world you live in.

"You have the power to create a loving world — you and others who send out loving thoughts. When you think beautiful, loving thoughts, you create beautiful,

loving things in your life.

"When you have a nightmare, let yourself wake up. Imagine yourself protected in God's white light, a bubble of armor all around you. Stand up and face the bear, lion or monster. Send it love, knowing you have the power to change it into anything you want. Imagine changing the bear to a puppy. Change anything you are afraid of to something you love, something soft and cuddly.

"Remember, the more fear you show, the more fear you will feel, and the bigger the monster you will create in your life. The more love you feel, the more love you give out, the faster the monster will disappear into pure light, pure love."

Peter assured Paul he would

practice the lesson every night. Peter was already feeling stronger, more sure of himself, more in control of the shadows.

Now, at last, he had a weapon —he would fight the creature in his dream with light and love. He would imagine the creature turning into a little puppy.

Yes, a puppy would be great!

If he dreamed of falling, he would imagine landing on a soft, pink cloud and floating safely back to Earth.

If he dreamed of a terrible war, he would imagine all the

weapons sending out love, making all the people feel loving and kind, dissolving all the anger and hate.

Peter knew the more he practiced what Paul had shared with him, the less fear he would have.

Peter knew that one day very soon he could truthfully say, "I'm not afraid of the dark . . . or anything else, either!"

List some of your own fears:

Using love and light, how can you change these fears so they will disappear forever?

Other Books by Leia Stinnett:

A Circle of Angels
The Twelve Universal Laws

The Little Angel Books Series:
The Angel Told Me to Tell You Good-bye
The Bridge Between Two Worlds
Color Me One
Crystals R for Kids
Exploring the Chakras
Happy Feet
One Red Rose
When the Earth Was New
Where is God?

All My Angel Friends (Coloring Book)

About the Author

The '80s were a decade of self-discovery for Leia Stinnett after she began researching many different avenues of spirituality. In her profession as a graphic designer she had become restless, knowing there was something important she had to do outside the materiality of corporate America.

In August 1986 Leia had her first contact with Archangel Michael when he appeared in a physical form of glowing blue light. A voice said, "I am Michael. Together we will save the children."

In 1988 she was inspired by Michael to teach spiritual classes in Sacramento, California, the Circle of Angels. Through these classes she had the opportunity to work with learning-disabled children, children of abuse and those from dysfunctional homes.

Later Michael told her, "Together we are going to write the Little Angel Books." To date Leia and Michael have created thirteen Little Angel Books that present various topics of spiritual truths and principles. The books proved popular among adults as well as children.

The Circle of Angels classes have been introduced to several countries around the world and across the U.S., and Leia and her husband Douglas now have a teacher's manual and training program for people who wish to offer spiritual classes to children. Leia and Michael have been interviewed on Canadian Satellite TV and have appeared on NBC-TV's *Angels II – Beyond the Light,* which featured their Circle of Angels class and discussed their books and Michael's visit.

The angels have given Leia and Douglas a vision of a new educational system without competition or grades — one that supports love and positive self-esteem, honoring all children as the independent lights they are. Thus they are now writing a curriculum for the new "schools of light" and developing additional books and programs for children.

Draw Your Guardian Angel Here: